PILLOW LACE AND BOBBINS

Jeffery Hopewell

Shire Publications Ltd

CONTENTS

Published in 1994 by Shire Publications Ltd, Cromwell House, Church Street, Princes Risborough, Buckinghamshire HP27 9AJ, UK. Copyright © 1975, 1977 and 1984 by Jeffery Hopewell. First edition 1975. Second edition 1977. Third edition 1984; reprinted 1985, 1987, 1990 and 1994. Shire Album 9. ISBN 0 85263 659 8.

Printed in Great Britain by CIT Printing Services, Press Buildings, Merlins Bridge, Haverfordwest, Dyfed SA61 1XF.

All bobbins, lace, parchments, pins and tokens are illustrated full size.

Two Pillow Horses

A bowed horse

A single horse

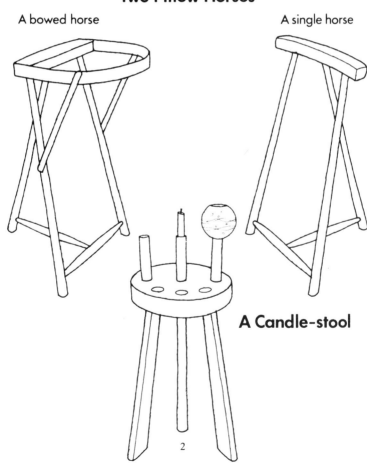

A Candle-stool

Part of a Honiton collar of a floral design. The flowers and leaves were worked individually and sewn together to form the complete article.

INTRODUCTION

It is not certain when, or by whom, pillow lace was first introduced to England. Local tradition has it that Queen Catharine of Aragon taught lace-making to some of the inhabitants of Ampthill when she resided there in 1531, and to give support to this an unusual lace of a Spanish style is made, known as 'Catharine of Aragon' lace. In addition the lace-makers kept Saint Catharine's day as a holiday, 'Catterns', and there is a stitch called 'Kat stitch' said to have been invented by her. Another theory is that Flemish immigrants, fleeing from persecution in the 1560s, brought the art of lace-making with them. The latter is more probable but there is no conclusive proof for either theory.

There are a number of references in the last quarter of the sixteenth century to 'bone lace', as it was then known, either because the bobbins were bone or because fishbones were used for pins. Shakespeare, in *Twelfth Night,* mentions 'the free maids that weave their thread with bones', which suggests that lace-making was sufficiently widespread for his audience to understand the allusion.

In 1596 the overseers of Eaton Socon engaged a woman to teach the poor children of the parish to 'worck bone lace', in an attempt to make them self-supporting. For this she was paid 2d for each child per week. From then on, references to the teaching of lace-making become more common, in the workhouses and lace schools. A lace school would be held in a room of the teacher's cottage where she would teach the youngest children and supervise the rest. In 1699, children of six or seven earned 20d a week, and a good adult would earn 6s 8d. The period of greatest prosperity was during the Napoleonic wars, when no foreign lace was being imported and exports to America were restored after the War of Independence. Both men and women made lace and earned up to 25s a week, and in one village, Hanslope, 800 people out of a total population of 1,275 were making lace.

There was a decline in the second half of the last century when machine-made lace improved and took over. In 1862 earnings had slumped, a child of six earned 4d a week and paid 2d of it for schooling, and a girl of fifteen earned only

3

1s, sometimes working twelve or fifteen hours a day. The industry never recovered from this blow and now lace-making survives only as a non-commercial hobby, which is once again becoming popular.

Lace was once made in a number of districts but there were only two of any great importance: Honiton and the East Midlands. In the latter, Bedfordshire, Buckinghamshire and Northamptonshire were the main lace-making counties along with the adjoining borders of Cambridgeshire, Hertfordshire, Berkshire and Oxfordshire. At one time lace was made not only in Devon but also in parts of Cornwall, Dorset and Somerset, but gradually the industry centred around Honiton, which gave its name to the lace and the whole district.

LACE

BELOW: *Three examples of Bucks point, which despite its name was made throughout the whole district and also in Devon, where it was known as 'trolly lace', from the Flemish 'trolle kant'. In Buckinghamshire a trolly is a bobbin (see page 24) which carries the gimp, a thick thread used for outlining the design, as in the lower two laces. The top lace is the 'Little Fan', usually the first lace a beginner learns as it is simple and requires only eleven pairs of bobbins. The parchment for the middle strip is shown on the front cover. The bottom lace has* *both point and honeycomb filling, but the ground is known as Kat stitch. The straight edge of the lace is called the 'foot' and the adjoining net the 'ground'. The curved edge is the headside, or turnside, which, if deeply scalloped, is sometimes called the dykeside. The names vary between different localities; for example, the small loops on the headside of the two lower laces are called picots (from the French), pearls (also spelt purls), headpins or turnpins.*

This photograph of a Buckinghamshire lace-maker was taken by Henry Taunt of Oxford in about 1900. She is making a Bedfordshire lace, using South Bucks bobbins, and her pillow is supported by an unusual type of pillow horse, sometimes called a 'maid' or 'lady'.

ABOVE: *Torchon lace. Torchon, in French, means a dishcloth or rag, a rather uncomplimentary name for this lace. It was rarely made in England until the end of the last century and was generally disliked by the old lace-makers, who preferred less geometric laces. Now, however, it is probably more popular than Maltese. The middle strip of lace, an insertion, is a sampler, with, from left to right, a whole stitch diamond, a half stitch diamond, five plaits, whole stitch with a raised plait and two spiders.*

OPPOSITE: *Maltese and Cluny lace. Maltese lace was first shown at the Great Exhibition of 1851 and was soon adopted by the English lace-makers. They could earn more at this lace, which was simpler and quicker to make than Bucks point. The next few years, until Maltese could be made by machine, were ones of comparative prosperity. It remained popular for some time and in 1919 it was estimated that whereas two or three people made Bucks point, fifty or a hundred made Maltese. It is often known as 'Bedfordshire Maltese', though it was made throughout the East Midlands. Cluny lace, so called after the old Italian lace in the Musée de Cluny, Paris, on which it was based, is similar to Maltese and was fashionable in the third quarter of the last century. The centre strip of lace is Cluny and the other two are Maltese.*

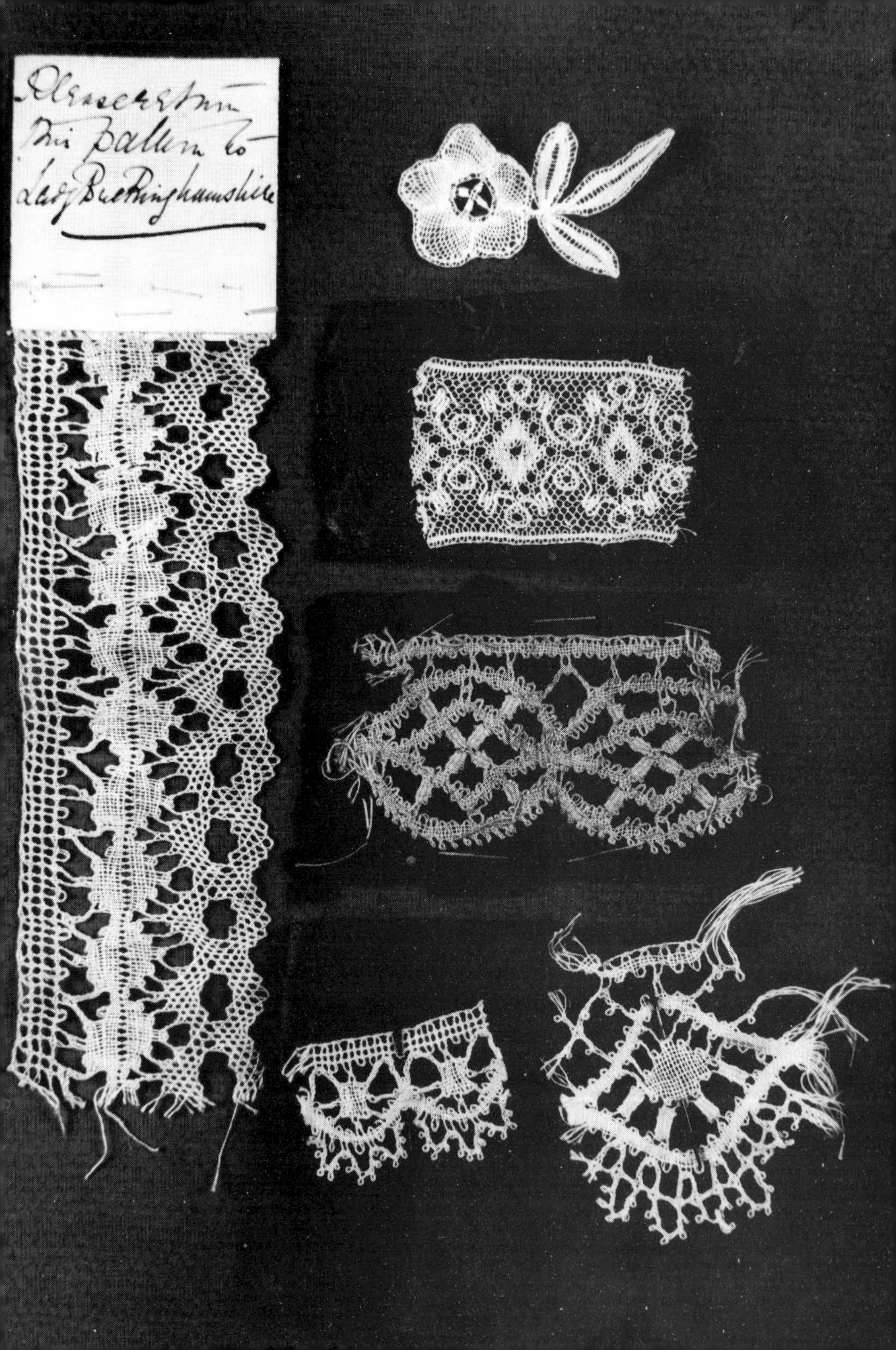
this pattern to
Lady Buckinghamshire

LEFT: *Five samples and a Honiton motif. The sample on the left belonged to the Countess of Buckinghamshire, who was one of the first to try to revive the industry in the 1880s. This pattern was sold at 1 shilling a yard. The other four are of humbler provenance, sewn or pinned on blue paper, and would be kept by a lace-maker to show a dealer or private customer the different designs she could make. The Honiton flower could either be sewn on a dress collar or wedding veil, made into a brooch or joined to others to make a larger item.*

ABOVE: *A lace dog, made for decoration, framed on a background of watered silk. Mrs Phoebe Lovell of Higham Ferrers used to make a number of similar keepsakes in the early years of this century. She would prick over a picture in the local paper or a photograph; amongst her more unusual designs were a running deer from a carving in Higham Ferrers church, a motif of Raunds church, and a picture of Elijah ascending to Heaven in a chariot of fire, all worked in lace!*

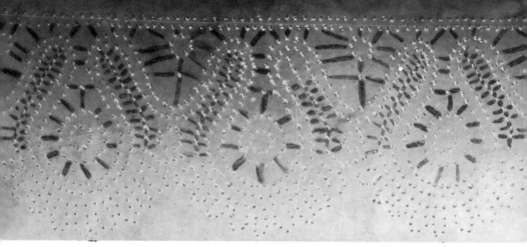

Two parchments. The pattern was pricked on to parchment from a draft on squared paper. The strip of parchment is usually about 14 inches long, with linen tabs, 'eaches', at both ends, so that it could be sewn to the pillow if the lace-maker wanted to make many yards of a particular pattern. The top parchment is for Maltese lace and the lower for Bucks point. Now it is difficult to obtain parchment, so a glazed cardboard is used.

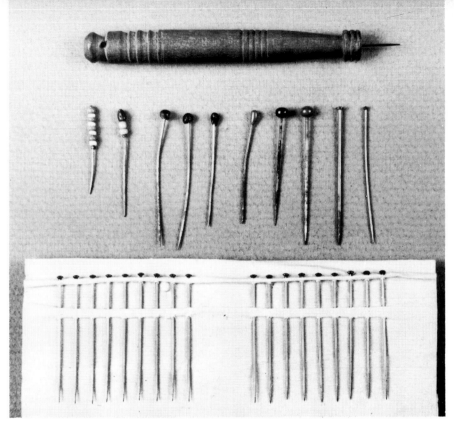

ABOVE: *A pricker, used for pricking the design on to a parchment. This one is a needle fixed into a broken bobbin.* In the old days a lace school would have a flat sheet of lead to do the pricking on, which could be melted down when it became too pitted and rolled flat again.

The pins used for lace-making are always brass, because they do not rust. In the early days of the industry, pins were expensive, 6s 8d per thousand in the sixteenth century, so the poor workers made their own from fishbones, in Devon, and thorns, in the Midlands. The pinhead was made separately and fixed on to the pin until 1824 when the solid-headed type was invented. This detachable head enabled the lace-makers to ornament a pin with little beads and push the head of another pin up the shank to keep them in place, as on the two on the left. These were called 'bugles' in South Bucks, 'limmicks' in North Bucks, 'kingpins' in Beds, or 'strivers', as they were sometimes stuck in a pattern to see how long it took to work them out again. The next two are 'hariffe pins', 'burrheads' or 'sweethearts', with burrs on the heads. The burrs would be soaked in milk or vinegar, depending on whether a light or dark colour was wanted. They would then swell, the skin could be removed, and the burr pushed over the pinhead, tightening as it dried. The middle two are capped with black or red sealing wax; a different colour would be used for the head and foot of the lace. The next two are glass-headed pins, usually imported from France, and the last pair are ordinary brass pins, the thicker for Maltese lace and the fine for Bucks point. Below is a paper of pins, something rarely seen today.

Pins are often mentioned in the 'lace tells' which were chanted by the children in the lace school as they worked.

'Nineteen little round holes
Gaping for a wire,
Every pin that I stick
Gets me one the nigher.'

The children had to stick ten pins a minute, and if they ran out of pins they would sing:

'Polly or Betsy a pin for the poor
Give me a pin and I'll ask for no more.'

There was always a pincushion hanging at the side of the pillow. It was usually stuffed with bran and was often shaped like a heart.

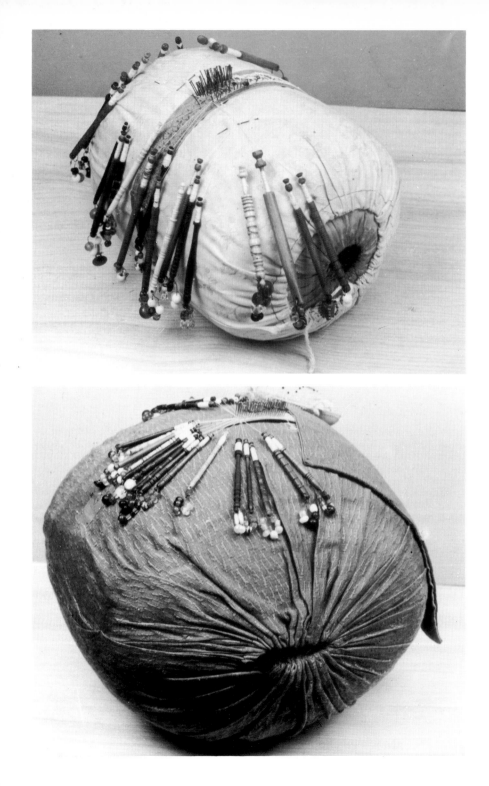

PILLOWS AND BOBBIN WINDERS

LEFT: *Lace pillows. These two show the different types used in the East Midlands. Occasionally a French pillow was used (see page 31) but these were generally scorned by the old workers. The top pillow is a 'round' or 'bolster' pillow, and the lower one a 'square' pillow. They were stuffed with straw until they were rock hard, in the same way as horse harness, using a mallet and dummy spike. They lasted a long time, some are still in use, but as the centre strip grew soft and the pins would no longer hold firm they had to be 'new-middled' every so often.*

The two pillows illustrated are not fully 'dressed', so that the shape can clearly be seen. The bottom one has a 'drawter' to cover the lace already made, and a pincushion. In addition it would normally have a 'worker' cloth to go under the bobbins and over the parchment, a bobbin bag with two compartments, for full and empty bobbins, and a small pair of scissors suspended on a chain. When not in use it would be covered by a 'heller' or 'hindcloth'. The bobbin second from the right on the top pillow has a 'bird-cage' spangle.

ABOVE: *A bobbin winder. Using a bobbin winder was much quicker than winding the thread on by hand. The skein of thread was stretched round the adjustable pegs on the crossed 'blades' or 'yarningles' and one end of it wound a couple of times round the neck of the bobbin, which was then put in the spool of the winder. The thread was wound on the bobbin as the fly-wheel turned. Winders, or 'turns', were usually made by local craftsmen, so there are rarely two alike, but they do not vary much from this principle.*

14

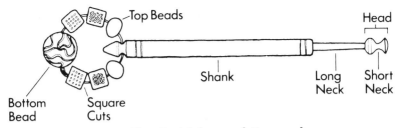

Top Beads · Head · Bottom Bead · Square Cuts · Shank · Long Neck · Short Neck

The Bobbin and Spangle

BOBBINS

The bobbins of the East Midlands are very beautiful and highly decorated. Unlike continental bobbins, each one is different from the next and one seldom finds two alike. Most of the bobbins seen today are from the nineteenth century. Few earlier ones survive, but one is inscribed 'Time flies 1714'. In this century a few have been hand-carved, but most were mass-produced and now modern plastic bobbins can be bought.

Bobbins are made of wood or bone, though occasionally of other materials. The wood was usually a close-grained hardwood, fruit wood being especially popular, which was sometimes taken from a special tree. One is inscribed 'Wakes Oak' from the tree traditionally associated with Hereward the Wake in Whittlebury Forest, which was burnt down in 1866. Bone bobbins are less common as they were more expensive, but they lasted longer. Brass, pewter and iron bobbins are very rarely found; they are always slim because of their weight. There are a few of ivory, but these would be far too expensive for the ordinary lace-maker, and most so-called ivory bobbins are in fact of bone, worn smooth from use. Glass bobbins were made, probably as a novelty for they are too fragile to use, but few now survive. Recently silver bobbins have been made, again not for use but for presentation.

All except the South Bucks bobbins have a ring of beads to give extra weight, add a bit of colour and keep the bobbin steady against the pillow. The bottom bead is usually larger than the rest and decorated; one type, grey with white spots and smaller red or blue spots on the white, is known as 'Kitty Fisher's eyes' after a famous eighteenth-century actress. Some of the others will probably be 'square cuts', which were impressed while hot with the side of a file. These are mainly red or white, occasionally dark blue and less frequently turquoise, amber, brown or green. The ring of beads is generally called the 'spangle' or occasionally 'jingle', a corruption of which, 'jinkum', is used in parts of Buckinghamshire and Oxfordshire. The wire on to which they are threaded is almost always brass, but copper wire and even string were used. The lacemakers sometimes put their own charms or mementoes on instead of beads: boot buttons, army buttons, shells, coins or anything with a hole in it. The 'bird-cage' spangle is made from a large bead surrounded by a number of strands of tiny beads. The large bead may sometimes be heart-shaped and is called a 'Valentine'.

Bobbins are usually 3½ to 4 inches long, excluding the spangle, though the author has one under 3 inches and another over 5½ inches. Some wooden ones are shortened because the friction of the spangle has enlarged the hole until the bottom breaks off, and another hole has to be drilled or burnt through with a hot wire higher up. Occasionally, a spangle was fixed by a small wire staple driven into the bottom of a wooden bobbin, but this broke off or wore through even more quickly.

LEFT: *Bobbin winders. The one above has a sliding lid in the base, making a drawer for bobbins, pegs or thread, and the winder below has a bent-wood wheel and thumb carving on the base. The holes in the blades are made to slope inward so that the pegs slope out to keep the skein in place. Pegs were frequently made from broken bobbins.*

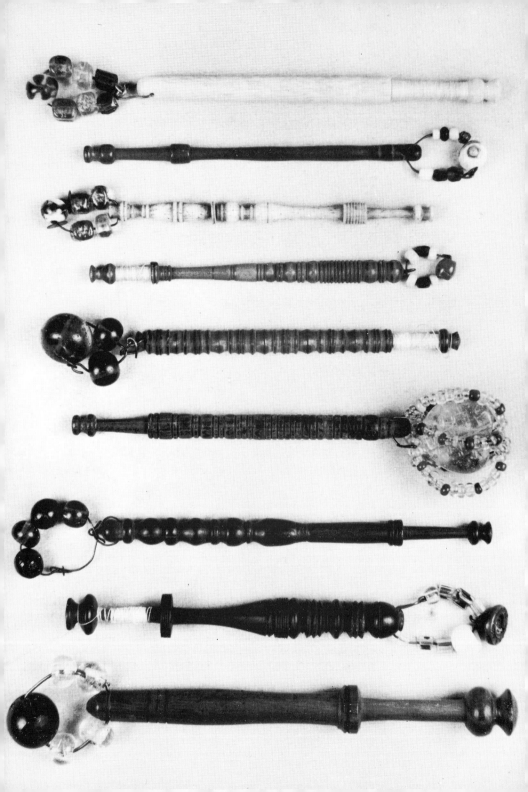

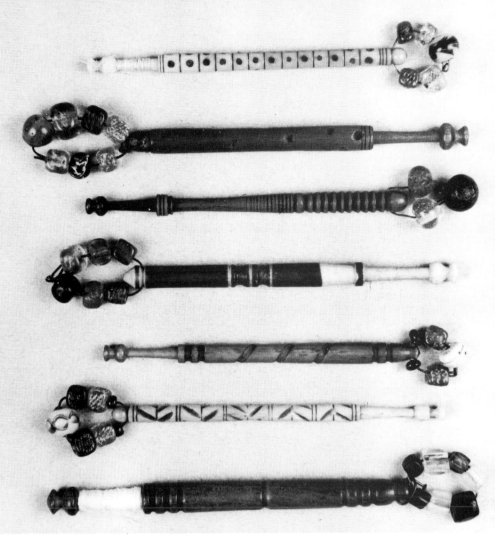

LEFT: *Turned bobbins. The top bobbin is bone, made in the 1930s when they cost 1s a dozen in wood, and 2s 4½d in bone, without spangles. The second is wood, a plain slim type known as an 'old maid'. The third is bone with a loose bone ring on the shank. The rest are wood; the next one has its spangle attached with a wire staple, and on the bobbin below the spangle is held on by an extra loop, a 'shackle'. This was more common in the south of the district, whereas in the north the wire of the spangle ran directly through the hole in the bobbin. The bottom bobbin is a heavy sort used for Maltese or the coarser Yak lace.*

ABOVE: *Bobbins with coloured decoration. From the top downwards: bone with green and red incised dots, a 'domino' bobbin; blue and red dots on wood; a wooden bobbin partly dyed green — the colouring is never very successful on wood because the dye does not penetrate deep enough and soon wears off with use; bone, dyed crimson with two gold bands in the middle of the shank; bone, green with red bands; red and yellow dashes on bone, two blue square cuts on the spangle; a wooden bobbin with red and blue rings.*

17

ABOVE: *Wire-bound bobbins. The top two are bone and the third wood, bound round with fine brass wire. Next is a tinsel inlay or 'fairing', with a strip of tinsel stuck in the spiral groove of the bone bobbin, which is also ornamented with brass wire. Below that are two wire-beaded bobbins, the first of wood with tiny orange, red and white beads, and the second of bone with red and blue beads. Lastly a bobbin that is an oddity and does not fall into any category. The head and neck are bone dyed green, five multi-coloured beads form part of the shank and the rest is bone with a hinged bone spangle.*

RIGHT: *The top bobbin is of pewter, and the rest have pewter inlay. The next two are 'leopards' with pewter spots that go right through the bobbins. Some have more than one form of decoration: pewter spots and wire binding or 'tiger' bands and wire. Below these is a bobbin with a broad pewter band, known sometimes as a 'tally'. The inscription that was punched on the band has since worn away. The two bone bobbins are 'tigers' but the lower one also has 'butterfly' decoration, which looks like an arrowhead. Next is a wooden 'butterfly' and finally a fancy design in pewter.*

18

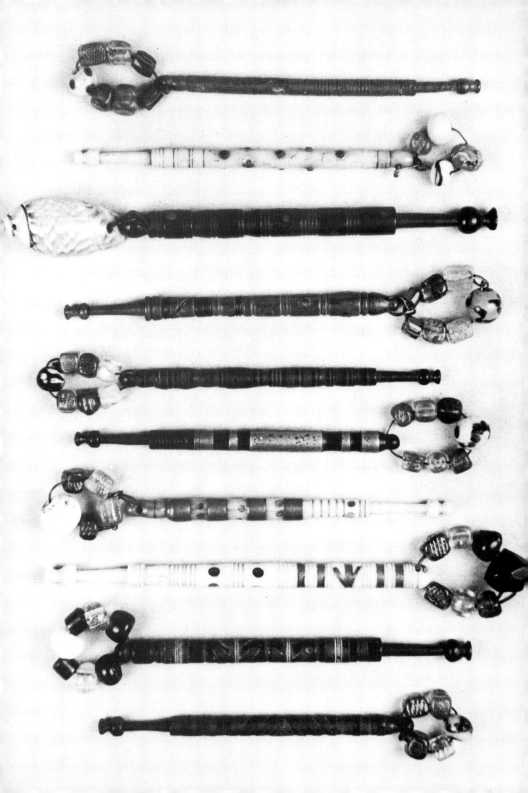

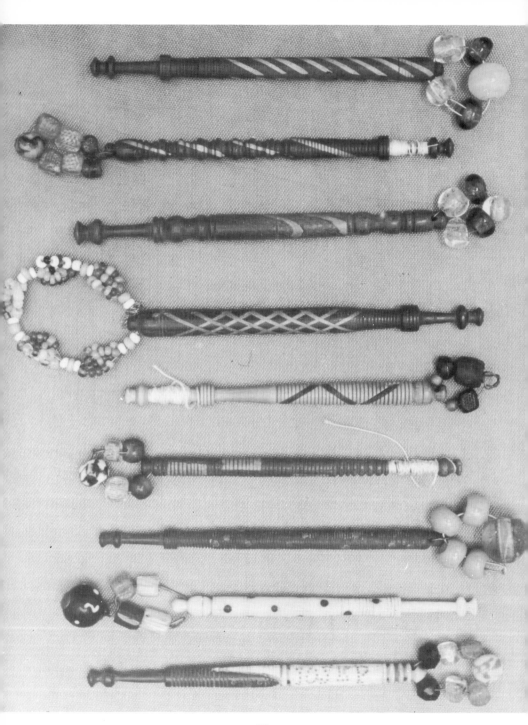

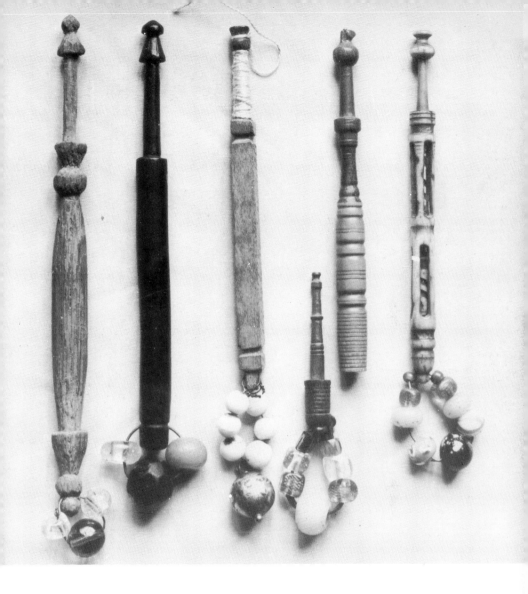

OPPOSITE: *Bitted bobbins. These are usually of dark wood inlaid with light, though occasionally light inlaid with dark are found. The strips were glued in, and often fell out with use. The spots on the bobbin third from the bottom are inlaid in a spiral pattern, whereas the dark wood spots on the bone one below go right through the bobbin. The bottom one of wood and bone is spliced and riveted with pewter and is inscribed 'Joseph', the bobbin maker having put the H on the other side.*

ABOVE: *The three bobbins on the left have not been turned on a lathe but hand carved with a 'shut-knife', often made by a young man for the girl he loved: a welcome gift, for a crude carved bobbin was just as functional as the two more elaborate ones on the right. Second from the right is a 'cow-and-calf' or 'jack-in-the-box', which pulls apart to reveal a baby inside, and that on the far right is a 'church window' or 'mother-in-babe', which has two tiny bobbins in the two tiers of four 'windows'.*

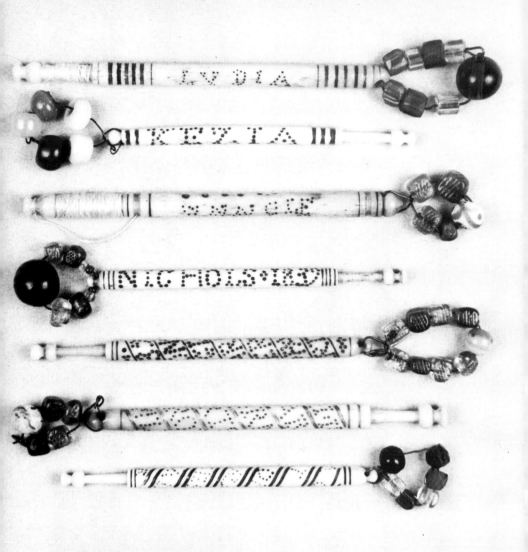

ABOVE: *Bobbins with Christian names were, not surprisingly, the most popular of all inscribed bobbins. The top two illustrated are 'Lydia' and 'Kezia(h)', but many different names are found, often old-fashioned like 'Alonzo' or 'Nehemiah', and some are mis-spelt: 'Charels' and 'Fredrick'. The names are sometimes prefixed with 'Dear' or 'Sweet' or a blessing: 'Bless my Jack'. Relationships are also mentioned; the next bobbin is 'Dear Unncle'. In addition to Christian names some have surnames, and, less frequently, dates:* 'Thomas Nichols 1839'. *A few have the name of the village as well:* 'Martha Parker Marsh Gibbon 1839'. *The next bobbin also has a spiral inscription:* 'Am(e)lia Roberts born March 21 1856'. *Others commemorate deaths:* 'Elisha Smith Goodman, born April 9 1824, died May 29 1843 aged 19 years'. *Bobbins were frequently given as presents, sometimes by the mistress of a lace school to a hard-working pupil. The last bobbin is inscribed* 'A gift from Frances Walker'.

22

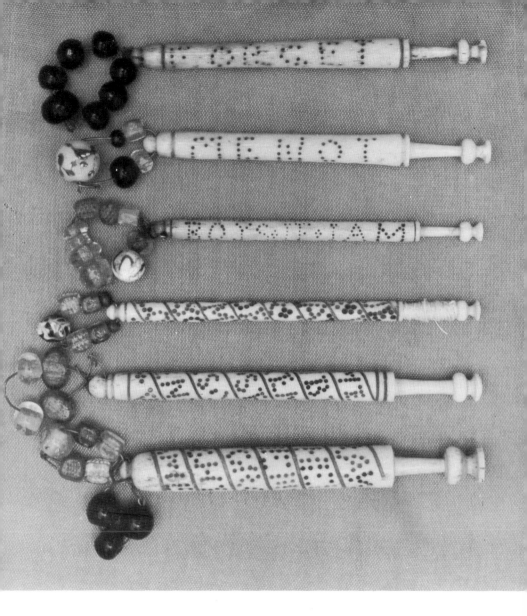

ABOVE: *Love and romance are frequently found on bobbins. The top two, both made by the same bobbin maker, are inscribed 'Forget me not'. The first one has a black spangle for mourning, suggesting that this romance may have ended unhappily. The third bobbin is inscribed 'Boys if I am raged, I am true', the maker having mis-spelt 'ragged'. The fourth 'I love you my dear that is true', the fifth 'When this you see* remember me', *and the sixth, which has two spangles, 'James Righton. Forget me not when far away'. Other similar inscriptions found on bobbins include 'My mind is fex(fixed) I cannot rang(e), I love my choice too well to chang(e)', 'Nothing but death shall part us too', 'Come and live happy with me my dear', 'A true hart will never change', and 'My love at a distant but ever in mind'.*

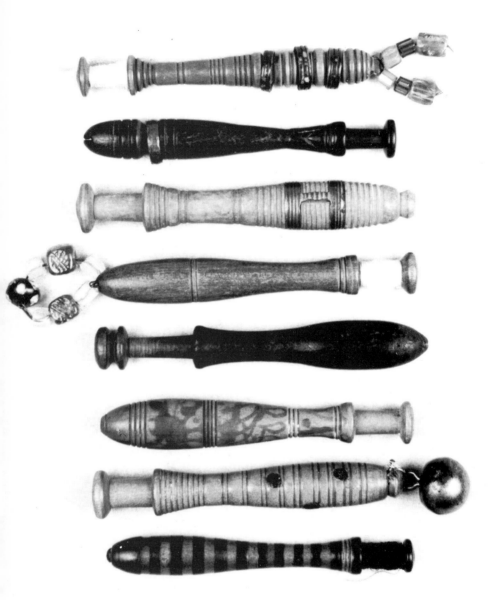

ABOVE: *South Bucks bobbins called 'Huguenots' or 'thumpers'. They are usually single-necked without spangles though three have had them added later, one with a wire staple. The top two are 'trollies' for gimp thread and have loose pewter rings, 'jingles', so that they can easily be distinguished. The lower one has an initial M carved on it near the neck. The next has an unusual pewter inlay. Third from the bottom is a bobbin stained with aqua fortis. Below that is a bobbin with spots of a darker wood let in and lastly one built up of alternate dark and light layers.*

HONITON

Honiton lace is made from separate motifs, 'sprigs', often of a floral design, which are either sewn on to a net ground or joined by a series of needle made bars. Although it is known as Honiton lace it was made over a wide area of East Devon. The industry was badly hit when Heathcoat established his factory for machine-made lace at Tiverton in 1816. Before then there were 2,400 lace-makers, whereas in 1822 there were only 300 and 1,500 people worked in Heathcoat's factory. Queen Victoria's wedding dress was made of Honiton lace, but even royal patronage was not enough to halt the decline and now lace is made for pleasure, not for a livelihood.

ABOVE: *Three bobbins or 'lace sticks'. These are pointed because they are passed through a loop of thread when connecting parts of the motif. Very fine thread is used so the bobbins have to be light to avoid breaking it. The top bobbin is stained with aqua fortis and the bottom one is decorated with diamonds, hearts, a crude flower in a pot, and the initials AM. Others have anchors, ships, fish or mermaids and some are inscribed with names, dates or mottoes.*

BELOW: *A Honiton pillow. This shape is convenient for sprigs, whereas a bolster pillow is better for lengths. The motif being worked is a flower design and a complete trefoil is shown pinned to the back of the pillow. A transparent 'slider', often a thin slice of horn, covered the lace already made to stop the thread catching on the pins.*

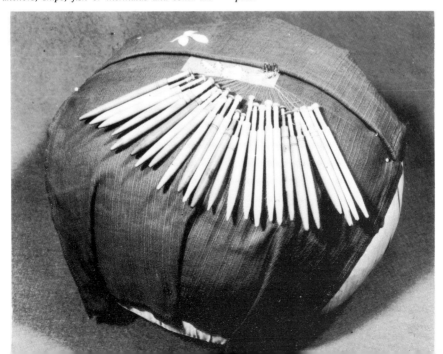

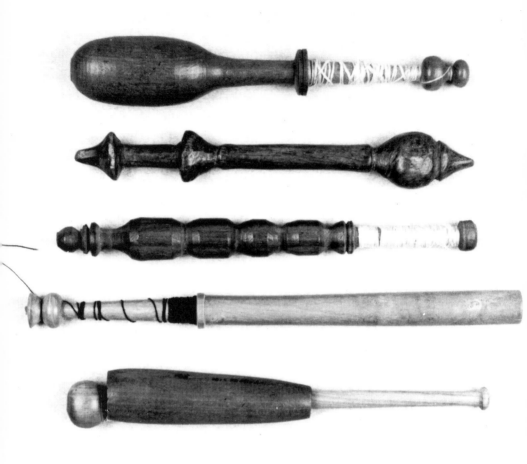

FOREIGN BOBBINS

Although none of the bobbins above is English, they were all found in Britain. The top one is French and was probably imported, costing 1 shilling a dozen in 1900, although some were made in England, usually with holes for beads. They would be used mainly for Torchon lace. The second bobbin is from Sri Lanka and was used for coarse laces. The pillow that the girls used was huge, the size of a large sack stuffed very hard, and propped up at one end while the girl squatted at the other end. Lace-making was originally taught by missionaries. The next

bobbin was bought from an old lady who had made lace as a child in Malta, and the bobbin below that is Spanish. The pillow used in both countries, and in Switzerland, is a long sausage shape and, instead of working around the pillow, the lace-makers work along the length. The last bobbin is Austrian, a type used in other countries as well, though very rarely in England. The bottom cover slips off, and the thread is wound round near the base and secured with a half-hitch at the neck, then the cover is replaced in order to keep the thread clean.

BELGIUM

Belgium is well known for its lace, especially pillow lace — Binche, Brussels, Mechlin and Valenciennes. Now Bruges is the main centre, and there is no danger of lace-making dying out for a flourishing lace school teaches both children and adults alike.

ABOVE: *Two bobbins. They are almost always of wood, sometimes dyed various colours. Similar bobbins can be seen in paintings of lace-makers by Vermeer, Netscher and other seventeenth-century Dutch artists.*

BELOW: *A lace pillow from Bruges at work on a Torchon pattern. The lower section of the pillow usually slides in the top but can be put at the bottom to allow the work to progress further down the pillow. It has two drawers, one at the back for the finished lace, and one at the side for bobbins etc. As always on the Continent, the footside of the lace is on the left and the head on the right, whereas in England the foot is on the right and the head on the left.*

FRANCE

In Normandy pillow lace was generally made in the coastal regions, mostly Blonde and Chantilly lace, whereas in the rest of the province the needlepoint laces, Point d'Alencon and Point d'Argentan, were made. The story goes that the lace-makers were so anxious to keep their lace clean that in winter, rather than have a smoky fire in the room, they would work in a room above a cow-shed so that the body heat of the cows would keep them warm.

BELOW: *An old postcard, dated 7th May 1904. of a lace-maker in regional costume. The lace pillow used is a large sloping desk with a revolving drum in the centre. The spare bobbins (below right) are kept in a small basket by her feet. Sometimes Normandy bobbins had a 'noquette' around the neck. This was a thin strip of horn or, later, coloured celluloid wrapped once around the neck with the two ends stitched together, which kept the thread clean.*

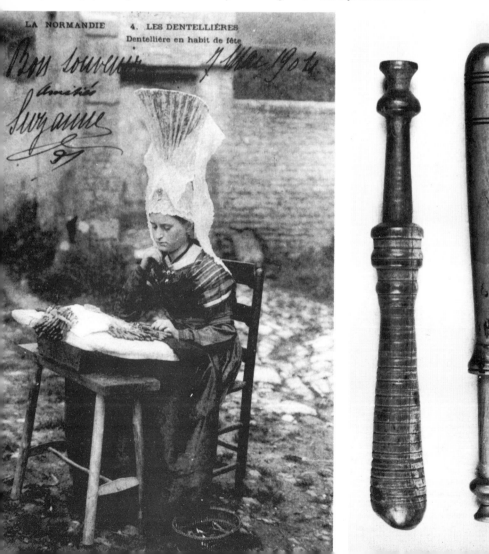

LA NORMANDIE   4. LES DENTELLIÈRES
Dentellière en habit de fête

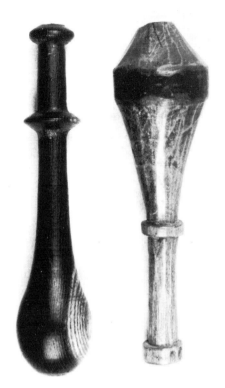

The lace-makers of Tignes were the most unusual of France. As can be seen from the postcard below, they used curious hoop-shaped pillows, which they gripped between their knees. The bobbins (left) are stout and hang over the side of the pillow, which gives greater tension. The laces made were coarse and unique in France for they were worked from memory and pins were only stuck at each edge. In other parts of the Alps the pillows were similar but the sides were of wood, decoratively carved, with a little door in one side, so that spare bobbins could be kept in the hollow centre. The bobbins too were frequently hand carved. Lace-making is now almost extinct in the Alps.

852. Costumes de la Savoie.
LES DENTELLIÈRES DE TIGNES.

The Auvergne lace-making district was centred around Le Puy. The lace made was generally Torchon, Maltese and Cluny, though some of the really skilled workers made superb Chantilly and Blonde laces. Lace-making has never completely died out and there is now a revival in this area.

ABOVE: *An old postcard of a lace-maker near Le Puy. Notice the pair of scissors hanging from her waist on a long chain. The pillow is always rested on the worker's knees, never on any kind of stand. The bobbin on the left is hand-carved and of a curious design. The other bobbin is a more standard type.*

OPPOSITE, ABOVE: *A bobbin winder. The bobbin is held between a spool-holder, smaller than the English, and a point on an adjustable screw. Some winders just hold the bobbin*

between two points and the driving cord is wound round the shank of the bobbin.

OPPOSITE, BELOW: *A pillow with a Torchon pattern in progress. This type of pillow is suitable for straight edgings. The parchment is pinned round a revolving drum so that the work can continue without the need to 'set up' again when the end of the parchment is reached. The French liked to use glass-headed pins for decoration though these often rusted. On the right is a lace-maker's lamp. The flask was filled with snow water and sometimes a few drops of sulphuric acid were added, giving the water a bluish tinge to soften the light. The oil lamp was put on the other side of the flask which concentrated the light on the lace being made. The English candle-stool, illustrated on page 2, also worked on the same principle. Four lace-makers, with four flasks, could thus work by the light of one candle.*

31

FURTHER READING

Buck, Anne. *Thomas Lester, His Lace and the East Midlands Industry 1820-1905.* Ruth Bean, Bedford, 1981.
Channer, C. C., and Roberts, M. E. *Lace-making in the Midlands.* Methuen 1900. (Reprinted in Buck, Anne. *In the Cause of English Lace.* Ruth Bean, Bedford, 1991.)
Earnshaw, Pat. *A Dictionary of Lace.* Shire Publications, 1982.
Earnshaw, Pat. *The Identification of Lace.* Shire Publications, second edition 1984.
Freeman, Charles. *Pillow Lace of the East Midlands.* Luton Museum, 1971.
Huetson, T. L. *Lace and Bobbins.* David & Charles, 1973.
Inder, P. M. *Honiton Lace.* Exeter Museums, third edition 1985.
Levey, Santina. *Lace – A History.* Victoria and Albert Museum/W. S. Maney, 1984.
Palliser, F. Bury. *A History of Lace.* Sampson Low, 1910.
Sharpe, A. M. *Point and Pillow Lace.* John Murray, 1913.
Springett, Christine and David. *Spangles and Superstitions.* Private, Rugby, 1987.
Springett, Christine and David. *Success to the Lace Pillow.* Private, Rugby, 1981.
Whiting, Gertrude. *Old Time Tools and Toys of Needlework.* Columbia University Press, New York, 1928; reprinted Dover Publications, 1971.
Wright, Thomas. *The Romance of the Lace Pillow.* 1919; reprinted Minet, 1971.

If the reader wishes to make lace then I recommend:
Nottingham, Pamela. *The Technique of Bobbin Lace.* Batsford, 1976.

The Lace Guild has been formed to promote lace-making of all descriptions and issues a quarterly magazine, *Lace*. Further details from The Lace Guild, The Hollies, 53 Audnam, Stourbridge, West Midlands DY8 4AE. Telephone: 0384 390739.

PLACES TO VISIT

There are many museums with collections of lace and lace-making equipment. Most are in the main lace-making areas. Here is a small selection:

Abington Museum, Abington Park, Northampton NN1 5LW. Telephone: 0604 31454.

Alby Lace Museum and Study Centre, Cromer Road, Alby, Norwich, Norfolk NR11 7QE. Telephone: 0263 768002.

Allhallows Museum, High Street, Honiton, Devon EX14 8PE. Telephone: 0404 44966.

Bedford Museum, Castle Lane, Bedford MK40 3XD. Telephone: 0234 353323.

Birmingham Museum and Art Gallery, Chamberlain Square, Birmingham B3 3DH. Telephone: 021-235 2834. The Pinto collection of wooden bygones.

Buckinghamshire County Museum, Church Street, Aylesbury, Buckinghamshire HP20 2QP. Telephone: 0296 88849.

Cecil Higgins Art Gallery and Museum, Castle Close, Bedford MK40 3NY. Telephone: 0234 211222.

Cowper Memorial Museum, Orchard Side, Market Place, Olney, Buckinghamshire MK46 4AJ. Telephone: 0234 711516.

Luton Museum and Art Gallery, Wardown Park, Luton, Bedfordshire LU2 7HA. Telephone: 0582 36941.

Museum of Costume and Textiles, 51 Castle Gate, Nottingham NG1 6AF. Telephone: 0602 483504.

Rougemont House Museum, Castle Street, Exeter, Devon. Telephone: 0392 265858.

The Story of Nottingham Lace, The Lace Hall, High Pavement, Nottingham NG1 1HN. Telephone: 0602 484221.

Victoria and Albert Museum, Cromwell Road, South Kensington, London SW7 2RL. Telephone: 071-938 8500.

COPING WITH

The Candida Albicans yeast infection can
cause total havoc in your body.

What are the symptoms?

How can you get rid of it?

How can you stay clear in the future?

Madison answers these questions in this clear,
practical handbook featuring simple diet and energy
medicine advice

CONTENTS

Hardly a week goes by without at least a couple of clients coming to me with Candida and it is a sobering reminder of just how common this clever little yeast is.

It masquerades under many different guises and is one of the most misdiagnosed 'complaints' in our modern society.

A trained Naturopath, Kinesiologist or Touch for Health[1] practitioner will be able to quickly test to see if you suffer from Candida. However, if you do not have access to such a professional, but suffer from some of the myriad symptoms set out on the next page, assume you have it and follow the programme for six weeks. Take time to observe carefully and evaluate your progress. You should feel a marked improvement in the symptoms by that time.

This programme enables you to put your health in good hands – your own! However, please use commonsense and if you have any concerns at all, consult your healthcare practitioner.

WHAT EXACTLY IS CANDIDA?

Candida Albicans is a parasitic yeast like fungus. We all have Candida, it exists happily in harmony in our body with other bacteria and yeasts BUT in certain conditions, it will begin to get out of control, to dominate and cause an infection – this is often referred to as Candidiasis and over time, can cause serious damage to any of your systems.

---

1 www.touch4healthkinesiology.co.uk for a list of UK practitioners
www.innersource.net for a list of worldwide EEM practitioners

It feeds on sugars and carbohydrates and as it gains in domination, releases toxins into the bloodstream which in turn can cause problems anywhere in the body but most commonly is found in the intestines, vagina, bladder or urinary tract. People make the mistake of thinking it is 'just Thrush' but it can be much much more than that.

In a normal gut there can be up to 4 lbs of live bacteria – a healthy balance would be 75% 'friendly' and 25% 'unfriendly'. When this ratio tips in favour of the 'unfriendlies' trouble begins.

Candida has increased greatly in recent years: our, sometimes indiscriminate, use of antibiotics can ultimately undermine our own body's immune function, at the same time stripping the friendly bacteria and creating an environment that is perfect for Candida to thrive. It is insidious and you may not feel the effects immediately, but if left unchecked, over the years, Candida Albicans [I'll call it CA from now on] can cause serious problems.

Unbelievably, many members of the orthodox medical profession do not yet recognise CA and its associated symptoms which are often diagnosed as some other condition, which, in fairness, is easy to do when you consider the symptoms. There is now a recognised medical test for CA and I am sure that as evidence mounts, more doctors will consider the possibility of CA in their diagnostic process.

In addition to prolonged use of antibiotics, other factors can 'tip the balance' and enable CA to get a foothold in the body:

1. Use of some medications such as the birth control pill, HRT and steroids and don't forget the antibiotics that lie hidden in our foods! [what was that chicken, cow or pig fed?].

2. A poor diet consisting of predominantly chemically-enriched convenience or processed foods, resulting in a toxic overload on the body. [don't get me wrong, I am immensely practical and occasionally resort to pre-packaged or prepared food, but the key word is 'occasionally'. Eating in this way should not be on a daily basis and please please please read the labels carefully; these marketing wizards are masters of creating the 'illusion' of a healthy product, read the label and it will often bring you smack bang back into reality.

3. Trauma, shock or stress of any kind.

4. Lowered immunity and general lack of 'balance' in the body.

5. Over consumption of drugs or alcohol.

Normally, following this anti-CA programme, you can regain a healthy balance again in about **four – six weeks.** However, in chronic cases it could take six months. After which it would be wise to be careful for a year, acknowledging that you may have a vulnerability to CA for a while.

The anti-CA regime is demanding, takes discipline and focus; the reality is that it is inconvenient, antisocial and sometimes a 'hard-slog', it would be dishonest and naïve not to face that reality but believe me, with a bit of organisation and creativity it becomes easier and it will, without doubt be worth it; you will never regret it. You will be amazed at the difference it can make to how you feel, physically and emotionally.

If you could put into a tablet all the benefits of this regime, it would be a best seller! It's a hard road but a worthwhile destination so:

- take a deep breath,

- take responsibility,

- take back control and

- take your very first step on that road – today!

THE SYMPTOMS

Because Candida can travel to various parts of the body, via the blood, the list of symptoms could be endless. However, below are some of the key symptoms. If you suffer from 3+ of any of these, chances are you have that little yeast devil feeding away somewhere in your body!

Bowel problems	Bladder problems	Headaches
Constipation	Heartburn	Earaches
Diarrhoea	Indigestion	Fatigue
IBS	Flatulence	Exhaustion
Abdominal pain	Bloating	Lethargy
Any stomach problem	Weight gain	Smelly feet
Bad breath	Cystitis	Irritability

'floaters' in the eye/s	Cravings for sugar	Toenail fungus
Night sweats	Allergies	Panic attacks
Any skin or nail issues	Itchy scalp, eyes, ears or patches anywhere on the body	Psoriasis – often misdiagnosed.
Loss of libido	Heart arrhythmias	anxiety
White spots in the mouth /tongue	Fungal infections such as Thrush	Stiff/aching muscles and joints
Memory loss	Inability to concentrate	Depression
Athlete's foot	eczema	Mouth blisters
General feeling of being 'spaced out'	Creamy patches on tongue	Sore inflamed tongue

 Symptoms will worsen in damp environments.

Here is a saliva test you can easily do at home – it's not 100% accurate but is interesting to do – best be alone when you do it.

First thing in the morning, **before you put anything in your mouth**, get a clear glass filled with water. Wiggle your mouth around to get a good dollop of saliva and spit it into the water. Come back to it 10/20 minutes later. If you have a problem with yeast, you will see strings (like legs) travelling down into the water from the saliva floating on the top, or "cloudy" saliva will sink to the bottom of the glass, or cloudy specks will seem to be suspended in the water.

If there are no strings and the saliva is still floating after at least one hour, you may well have no yeast problem.

The critical key to 'curing' Candida is taking a good long look at your diet and making any changes that are required.

What you will have to eliminate for a few weeks, is probably some of, what you consider to be, your basic 'staple' foods – it can be difficult and requires motivation, discipline and organisation; you will be changing deeply rooted habits.

Let me say right now, I am not being negative or pessimistic, rather realistic in assessing the challenge. If you know what you are up against, you will not be discouraged at the first hurdle, you will know it is normal, you are not a 'failure' if you trip up some days. Taking it one step at a time will yield a positive outcome.

One of my favourite quotes is by Bob Hoskins in Maid in Manhatten: **"What defines you as a person is not that you fall down, it is how quickly you get up".**

Yes, aim for the stars, aim for being 100% perfect on this regime but do NOT beat yourself up and walk away from it just because you fall down occasionally. Tomorrow is another day, another blank piece of paper upon which to write your story – make it a good one!

A little technique I find useful is:

Tap the apex of both your cheeks with your middle fingers. Smile widely and say:

"I'm doing this, I'm doing this well and I am winning – all is well"

Say it three times while tapping whenever you need a bit of support, whenever you might be feeling a bit sorry for yourself – there is power in your thoughts and words so observe your vocabulary and start making it positive from now on. Acknowledge the challenge but affirm that you are up to it and are indeed a winner!

The right frame of mind is imperative, take the attitude that you are investing in your well-being not just now, this year, but in the years to come. CA, unchecked, does *not* go away, it grows and so do the problems associated with it.

The anti-CA regime involves eliminating the foods it feeds on. This is a siege, there is *no* easy way – you have to starve the little yeast devil out!

The foods it likes are those that contain:

- **Sugar**
- **Yeast**
- **Gluten**
- **Some carbohydrates** [they turn to sugar]
- **Moulds**
- **Chemicals and antibiotics**
- **Anything that 'ferments'**

So, the elimination list would include:–

Sugar	Sweeteners – all of them. Use Savia.	Honey
Carbohydrates	Malt (form of sugar)	Preserved foods
Processed foods	Refined foods	Gluten breads
Wheat	Barley	Rye
Yeast baked goods	Stock cubes	Malt extract speads
Cereals containing malt, sugar, chemicals	Msg – often found in chinese food	Some tinned foods, e.g. Baked beans – check ingredients list to see if the can contains sugar.
Supplements that contain yeast	Anything from the cow	Smoked, dried, pickled or cured foods
Cheese	Mushrooms	Tomatoes – see notes
Nuts	Peanut butter	Cured ham / bacon
Soy products when they are genetically modified	Chocolate *[don't hate me too much!]*	pork
Soy sauce	Dried fruits	Pickles
Chutney	Mayonnaise	Horse-radish
Tomato sauce	Fruit and juices	popcorn
Tea	Coffee	Fizzy drinks
Processed meats	shellfish	Most farm raised fish
Alcohol – all of it I'm afraid. It is fermented.	Vinegar – except apple cider	Hot spices (irritate)

FRUITS – sorry, yeasts like fructose. Fruits such as oranges and grapefruits seem acidic but they are alkaline forming and Candida loves them! Try to eliminate totally, if you feel the need, try banana, kiwi or apple.

Lemons and limes are allowed in small quantities.

Limit your intake of potatoes, yams and corn [starch/sugar] – again, self test to see how your body chemistry gets on with these foods [shown later in the book].

Tomatoes – vary greatly on where they are grown, how they are grown and body chemistry. Avoid them if you have high uric acid levels, otherwise test to see how your body processes them.

Get creative and organised – it is critical in those first few weeks that you starve the Candida and 'kill' off the excess, restoring a healthy balance of intestinal flora.

Don't sit around feeling depressed about it all: go to the gym, for a walk, clear out the loft ... Keep busy and keep your mind off the subject of food!

Where possible impose an eating 'curfew' at 6pm. This lessens the stress on the digestive system during the night.

The above list is a generalisation that has emerged over years of observation by healthcare practitioners. However, our body chemistries are all different and to honour that individuality you could self-test foods to see if your body can metabolise them efficiently or not [in which case they will stress your body and reduce your immunity].

Self testing allows you to truly eat to match your body chemistry. Just think, you need never have to be confused again by conflicting 'reports' on different foods – simply test and see what is the truth for you. This is a simple yet powerful tool.

Take a look on You Tube – tap in Madison King self testing and you will see me demonstrating 3 different self-testing techniques.[2] Try each one and see which you find the most effective, comfortable and easiest, then stick with that one and practise, practise, practise: after a while you will gain confidence and trust in the tests and can truly fine tune your eating to support rather than sabotage your body.

It has to be said you can influence these tests if you choose to. Be sure that you are feeling as objective and neutral as possible. Tell yourself you are seeking the truth, knowledge and any interference would only be self sabotage. That once you have the truth it is entirely your choice what you do with that information.

---

2 Also available on my DVD – Madison King Food Testing Made Simple, available on my website www.midlifegoddess.ning.com_

You will be using your body as a pendulum: stand, barefoot if possible, feet solidly on the floor, not too far apart, knees unlocked, take a deep breath, set the intention that you want an honest dialogue with yourself.

Place one hand over your solar plexus and the other hand over the first. It doesn't matter which one.

Tuck your elbows into your sides.

Close your eyes and say "*my name is Minnie Mouse*". Now, does your body sway forward or backward?

Repeat the test but this time saying "*my name is [your name]*" – what happens?

Normally the body will sway forward toward the truth or a substance that is strong/positive and easily metabolised and backward i.e. away from one that is weak/negative, does not suit the body chemistry, or an untruth [avoid the latter].

It will either be attracted or repelled. You will sway forward or backward.

However, rules are always made to be broken and some people reverse the sway. You may even vary occasionally. By using the Minnie Mouse test you can establish your personal weak and strong sway for that day.

11

<u>WITH FOODS</u>: simply hold the sample against the solar plexus or navel and see in which direction you sway. Normally a forward sway indicates your body will tolerate that food and a backward sway that it is better to eliminate the food from your diet, at least for ten days and observe how you feel.

It is always better to hold the food directly in your hand or in a glass dish. Plastic can sometimes give a false reading.

THE STICK TEST

No, this is not me playing shadow rabbits!

The stick test was shown to me by Dr Michael Burt ND[3]. It is so discreet it can be used anywhere, anytime. In fact, a friend of mine who has been using it for years, can test the menu at any restaurant she visits, using this technique. Nobody realises she is selecting the healthy choice for her body.

Centre yourself and take a deep breath, relax and rub the pads your index finger and thumb together, naturally, no real pressure. Now, as before, say "my name is Minnie Mouse" and observe what happens, do the fingers slide together more easily, or do they feel a little more 'sticky'? Repeat using your own name and observe what happens.

---

3 A truly remarkable naturopath in London – www.brabandhouseclinic.co.uk

If you feel a marked difference, then this is a great test for you to practise as it is so easy and unobtrusive. Normally sliding more easily indicates a positive and feeling more friction, a certain 'stickiness' indicates a negative.

THE QUAD TEST

Testing the quadriceps muscle is not quite as convenient, but it is easy and reliable, a really solid technique: sit straight on a chair, with feet firmly planted on the ground in front, the chair should neither be too high nor too low. Lift one leg slightly off the chair. Now, with the heel of your hand, press down on that knee, while the knee resists. If the leg stays locked take it as a strong result but if the leg goes down easily then it is a weak result.

WITH FOOD – place sample against solar plexus or navel and do the test, does the leg stay locked [positive result] or does it weaken and you are able to push it down to the floor [negative result]

Go to a sports store and head for the weightlifting section. Find a dumbbell that you can hold out in front of you with effort. Hold it out and think a happy, vibrant thought[4]– does it feel easier to hold? Now think of something negative or depressing – is it now hard to hold? You need to select the weight that gives you this result.

Instead of a dumbbell, you can use bottles of water in a bag and one of my clients has a really cute little wicker basket [with handle] that she fills with pebbles to get exactly the right weight.

Test it out: place the weight on a shelf at shoulder height. Hold a sugar cube in one hand. Stand in front of it and with other hand try to lift it. The energy of the sugar cube will affect the energy running through the muscle and it should be difficult to lift. Repeat with something you know your body likes, or say your name [my name is...] and it should be easy to lift, thus indicating a strong test.

---

4 Thoughts generate subtle energies that affect our bodies. We can use this to our advantage in gauging the weight of the dumbbell but of course it has far reaching implications – don't harbour toxic thoughts or you will be weakening your body.

An interesting aspect of this concept is developed by the renowned Japanese scientist, Masaru Emoto in his book The Hidden Messages in Water.

Because dumbbells exert a steady pressure downward [gravity], they provide a reasonably objective testing technique. It is important that you find the correct weight. Too light, or too heavy will reduce accuracy.

If you do not have a suitable shelf available, simply hold the weight by your side and see if you can pull the arm away from the side of the body.

So, with a combination of the list and self testing you can determine the best foods to eliminate from your diet. That knowledge can be invaluable in your return to health.

SO, WHAT ON EARTH IS LEFT THAT YOU CAN EAT ?!

Raw/steamed VEGETABLES *they absorb and help eliminate fungal poisons. Green beans, spinach and broccoli are the best.*	Garlic, onion, leeks and chives contain anti-fungal properties	Free range **chicken.** *[Free from hormones, antibiotics or chemicals]*
Fish – try and get organic fish not farmed	Tinned tuna[5]	Tinned sardines *[if fresh are not available]*
Home made humus	Maize crackers	Yeast/gluten free stock cube
Lamb	Olive oil – cold pressed	Brown rice

5 But not too much Tuna if you have high Uric Acid levels.

Millet	Rice cakes	Oat cakes
Rye pumpernickel (gluten free)	Original RYVITA	Alfalfa sprouts – but rinse well
Avocado	Tofu	Salad
Porridge oats	Coconut milk	Sheep's milk
Goat's milk and cheeses	Blue corn / corn chips	Seeds (sunflower, sesame, pumpkin)
Gluten free pasta	Coconut oil Anti fungal	Herbs and spices
Lentils	Pulses	Organic live goat or sheep yoghurt
Herb teas – camomile and peppermint are particularly good	Rooibosch tea – must be organic and test yourself first	**Filtered or bottled mineral water – aim for 2 litres daily**

All foods to be organic and fresh – not always possible to achieve, or available... but try your best within your own individual financial/time restraints.

Organic live yoghurt can be applied directly to the vagina if you are suffering Thrush – try it straight from the fridge, very calming.

There are now many recipe books on Candida – search around and get some inspiration to avoid total boredom.

Allergies should decrease with this regime. However be wary of any foods you suspect might represent an intolerance – energy test them first.

In fact, my basic rule is:
If in doubt, energy-test the food.

I am the world's worst cook, but here are some of my easy and quick ideas to get you started. With a little creativity, your diet can be varied and interesting.

If you discover some tasty, simple dishes, please let me know and I will include in the next revision to this eBooklet.

	BREAKFASTS

Where possible serve in a glass rather than a bowl –
for some reason it not only looks but also tastes better!
Try it.

1. Organic porridge oats with cinnamon, banana and goat's milk. Either hot or made the night before and eaten cold from the fridge.

2. The Walled Garden Special [*with thanks to Anna*] – I simply love this one: Chop up a banana and put into the base of the glass, add a tablespoon of linseed or split hemp seed, pour over some natural soy yogurt [some brands have a delicious vanilla tinge to their taste][6] or Greek goats yogurt; sprinkle with a dessertspoonful of crispy muesli [make sure it's sugar/wheat free] or toasted puffed rice. When you no longer have CA you can add chopped kiwi fruit or

---

6 Always read the label, you may be surprised how many so called 'natural' foods have added sugar – if the white devil features in the top 3 of any list then put that product back on the shelf!

berries for a real treat. A pinch of desiccated coconut adds a tasty finishing touch.

3. Chopped apple and walnuts with cinnamon and goat/soy yogurt.

4. Banana smoothie: banana, goats milk, ice, 1 raw egg, ¼ teaspoon of rosewater. Blitz and enjoy.

5. Live goat's/sheep's yoghurt with banana and cinnamon topped with a sprinkle of desiccated coconut.

6. Puffed brown rice, goat's milk and diced banana

7. Wheat/gluten free muesli

8. Freshly juiced vegetables – eg carrot

9. Rice with cinnamon and nutmeg (my guilty secret is to make a batch of this, divide into containers and leave in the fridge, whip up and enjoy at any time of day.) Use Stevia to sweeten.

10. Scrambled eggs and gluten free rye pumpernickel bread or Ryvita

11. Boiled eggs and ryvita

12. Kedgeree

 Cinnamon is an infection fighter and kills bacteria and fungi

1. CHICKEN BREAST [grilled] and salad – spice up the chicken with garlic/herbs etc.,

2. Lemon gingered chicken with vegetables, onion, leeks or brown rice. This recipe was given to me by Paul and is one of my staples:

    Into a large pan pour a couple of tablespoonfuls of olive oil and add ground turmeric, black pepper, diced ginger, crushed garlic, ground pimenton dulce, tamari sauce – a few shakes[7] and a finely diced onion, chopped chicken, blend and cook until the onion is soft. Add juice from half a lemon [and half the lemon] two handfuls of rice and mix so the rice is coated. Add enough water to fully cover the rice, bring to boil and then simmer until the rice is cooked. Remove the lemon rind and let stand before eating.

    I tend to make a batch of this, divide into containers and keep in the fridge. When I want to use it, I heat in a non-stick pan and add one egg, mixing in vigorously to make my very own, egg fried rice!

    You can leave out the chicken or replace it with prawns or fish of your choice.

    I can't believe I am typing this, I am such a bad cook so I promise you, if I can do this anyone can!

---

7 Avoid Soya sauce

3. Chicken and broccoli stir fry, but remember, no Soya Sauce.

4. LAMB and salad. Roast the meat and tear into strips and add to your salad.

5. Marinated lamb kebabs – marinade in fresh herbs of your choice and olive oil [put in a plastic bag in the fridge for a few hours]. Grill and serve with rice of fresh green salad.

6. FISH and salad. I often cook my fish in tin foil with just a twist of lemon and pinch of herbs, one of my favourite being tarragon.

7. Tuna or sardines with brown rice and vegetables

8. Rainbow trout and vegetables or salad

9. Smoked salmon on gluten free rye pumpernickel bread with twist of lemon and black pepper

10. Poached salmon and broccoli

11. Brown rice and vegetable stir fry

12. Baked potato and steamed vegetables

13. Baked potato + humus and salad

14. Baked potato + avocado dip and salad

15. Courgette risotto

16. Spanish omelette + goats cheese (occasionally)

17. Soups: watercress + potato / leek + potato / Parsnip / root veggies / carrot + coriander. Courgette and onion. Add toasted seeds and/or pine nuts.

SNACKS

1. Seeds

2. Avocado

3. Ryvita + smoked salmon, pepper and lemon (as a treat you may add a little soft goats cheese)

4. Hard boiled egg + Ryvita (easy and very portable)

5. Rice pudding: mix a cup of cooked brown rice with 2 tablespoons of coconut oil and pinch of cinnamon and some stevia to sweetener.

6. Omelette – onion and spinach. Can be eaten hor or cut into squares and eaten cold as a snack.

7. Raw vegetable sticks + hummous

8. Tabbouleh (careful, no vinegar)

9. Yoghurt + cucumber, garlic, lemon and mint

10. Grated carrots + sesame seeds

11. Avocado and prawns on Ryvita or gluten free rye pumpernickel bread

12. Wheat/gluten/yeast-free cookies (you'll find in specialist health-food stores – try them all to find one you like, sometimes you have to kiss a few frogs before you find your prince.)

13. Ryvita + tuna and black pepper

14. In a blender, mix tuna (or avocado) with yoghurt, lemon and black pepper

Use as a spread on Ryvita or gluten free rye pumpernickel bread.

15. Tahini blended with lemon juice, garlic and black pepper – delicious with Ryvita or crudités.

The secret is to get creative, devise your menus and enjoy all the foods and tastes that you are allowed. Dig out your cookbooks and do a Google for Candida recipes. http://candidarecovery.com/recipes/recipes.htm#chicken and http://www.foodforthoughtuk.com/expertadvice/anticandidarecipes.php are just two examples of what you can find and for you cooks out there, you will rise to the challenge magnificently I am sure!

Don't start feeling you are being denied and 'poor me', rather think how wonderfully empowering it is to KNOW there is something YOU can do to help you on the road to recovery... Come on YOU CAN DO IT, just get organised.

Remember, when the yeast starts to 'die-off' you may experience an *increase* in your symptoms and perhaps headaches, nausea and skin eruptions or itchiness.

Do not be alarmed.

If you are sticking to the 'regime' and not cheating, this should be considered a 'good-sign' that the programme is working.
It will pass ... Consider it the storm before the calm!
Drink plenty of water and perhaps some milk thistle to speed elimination.
If you have access to a sauna or steam room –
use it to aid elimination through sweating.

If you find the going hard, use a well established energy medicine technique to help you stick with it:

Tap a acupoint on the top of your hand [doesn't matter what hand] for 5 seconds, breathing deeply and saying: *"I can do this, I can do this – I am doing this, I am doing this – all is well, all is great – well done little 'ole me".* So, if you decide to follow the anti CA regime and are finding it, shall we say a challenge: tap this point [while repeating the affirmation] and it will help you ride the temporary wave of hunger or craving.

It takes down the stress around the issue which provides you an opportunity to 'choose' how you react, rather than be driven by that stress. Smile while you tap, it increases the efficiency of any technique.

Useful in other areas of your life too, wherever you want to recruit a calming 'helping hand'. Often used successfully when coping with a phobia such as acrophobia.

So where is the point? place one finger between the knuckles of little and ring fingers, then move towards the wrist about ¾" or until you arrive at a natural little indentation – this is the 3rd point on the Triple Warmer flow.

SUPPLEMENTS TO SUPPORT YOUR PROGRAMME

- Use tinctures wherever possible, they provide slightly better absorption

- Hunt out 'yeast-free' versions of the supplements

- Some reputable manufacturers, such as Higher Nature,[8] do 'blends' specifically targeting Candida. Make sure they are good quality and energy test to see if they are right for your personal body chemistry.

8 www.highernature.co.uk

Choose **one** of these supplements.	**PAU D'ARCO** – the inner bark of a South American tree, has anti-fungal properties.
	Also known as Taheebo or Lapacho
Combined with the diet, they form a potent partnership to kill off the yeast invaders.	**CAPRYLIC ACID** – fatty acid in coconuts – anti-fungal properties.
	CALCIUM MAGNESIUM CAPRYLATE 400 mg daily is anti-fungal and has good absorption
	GARLIC – broad spectrum anti-fungal. Check it contains ALLICIN
	GRAPEFRUIT SEED EXTRACT
	COLLOIDIAL SILVER – anti bacterial/viral

At the same time you could consider strengthening the Liver while it is dealing with the increased toxic waste with Milk thistle

	Psyllium Husks will help cleanse the gut
Gut repopulation is a must.	**Acidophilus** – this is a 'live' supplement and should be kept in the fridge after opening. Again look at some of the combos that are now on the market. Take a look at Higher Nature's site for some good options.
IMMUNE builders These will be taken for a couple of weeks only, after that a good general multi vitamin and mineral should be sufficient.	**Echinacea** **Cats Claw** – try the tea **Astragalus** – good for respiratory tract **Zinc** – 50mg daily, taken alone at night **Vit C** – 3 gms daily And of course some of the combos available
DIGESTION AIDS	Higher Nature's Digestive Enzymes BioCare Digestive Enzymes Easigest

For a couple of weeks to ensure the gut heals; your choice is wide. Here are some ...	**Aloe Vera** – also a powerful anti-fungal **Slippery elm** **Linseed** oil – I mix these [or split Hempseed] into my breakfast muesli and yogurt in the mornings **Olive oil** – contains Butyric acid which helps healing of intestinal wall. **Coconut oil** **Tea Tree** Oil. Use as a gargle and pop a couple of drops in your bath. Anti-fungal.
General strengthening with a good quality vitamin and mineral. One of my favourites is **Pure synergy** – energy test first as it contains mushrooms + is very expensive, but well worth it.	

You are putting all this time, effort and money into getting yourself well, I would suggest, if you have a good nutritionist near to you, book an appointment, the advice you receive on supplementation will be invaluable. Take a look at Patrick Holford's site – Optimum Nutrition for cutting edge information www.patrickholford.com and the Institute of Optimum Nutrition for advice on finding a practitioner. www.ion.ac.uk

LIVER CLEANSE EVERY MORNING

Before you go to bed at night, prepare a large glass of water into which you add a small piece of lemon. Cover the top of the glass and keep it by your bed. When you wake, before you do anything else, drink the room temperature water. It will help 'flush out' the liver. [use unwaxed, organic lemon].

SPINAL FLUSHING

We are all familiar with the body's lymphatic system, garbage disposal at its best, key to our immunity, helping counter conditions ranging from colds to cancer and definitely your friend in the battle with CA.

The lymphatic system is bigger than the circulatory system, but does not have a heart to pump the lymph around the body, it relies on gravity and exercise/ movement. With our increasingly sedentary lifestyles, the system can become sluggish and less effective in clearing toxins from certain parts of the body. When this happens the 'garbage' can accumulate and cause very real problems.

To maintain a healthy lymphatic system: move, walk, body brush, drink water, get a massage and a daily 'Spinal Flush'.

"What is a Spinal Flush?" I hear you ask. It is simply a firm massage along either side of the spine. Through clothes or directly on skin, it stimulates certain 'neurolymphatic reflex points' that trigger the garbage disposal system into activity and encourage the efficient removal of toxins from the body and strengthen immunity.

You will feel more energized and optimistic as the body begins to rid itself of stagnant energies and emotional residue. It also stimulates the cerebrospinal fluid, clearing your head. If you feel the very first signs of a cold coming on, a Spinal Flush can stimulate your immunity enough to nip it in the bud. In fact, if you did this every day to each other, you may not even catch a cold in the first place!

It is a great technique for partners as it quickly dissolves built up stress and takes the edge off any 'emotional overreaction' [an understated way of saying things getting a little heated and you are about to either become a foulmouthed fishwife, go into a tight lipped sulk or flounce out the door!]. So, rather than head towards an argument and divorce proceedings, give each other a spinal flush, an inexpensive form of marriage counselling without words!

If any of the points feel sore, unless there is an obvious reason, such as a bruise, injury or medical condition, the soreness indicates that the point, and its corresponding organ, need a bit of attention, so linger on the point a little longer. However, if you are recovering from an illness or suffer an autoimmune problem, you may find a lot of the points are sore. If this is the case, go easy so as not to overwhelm the system.

To do the Spinal Flush takes about a minute, but is so enjoyable you may well be pleading 'don't stop!'.

Lie face down, or stand 3-4 feet from a wall and lean into it with your hands supporting you at chest level. This positions your body to remain stable while your partner applies pressure to your back.

Your partner massages the points down either side of your spine, using the thumbs, fingers or knuckles [if you have nails knuckles are by far the best option].

Apply body weight to get strong pressure but no rough, jerky or sudden movements.

Massage from the bottom of the neck all the way down to the bottom of the sacrum. Go down the notches between the vertebrae and deeply massage each point for a few seconds, moving the skin in a circular motion with strong pressure but ensuring that the pressure is comfortable. This technique should not feel painful. Make sure neither of you are holding your breath.

Upon reaching your sacrum, your partner can repeat the massage or complete it by 'sweeping' the energies down your body, from your shoulders, and with an open hand, all the way down your legs and off your feet, 2-3 times.

Each of these points relate to a specific energy meridian/ organ but do not be concerned about missing one, just work between all the notches and give a little extra time to any that feel 'sore'.

I suppose I should say, please use your common sense and do not do a Spinal Flush if there is even a whisper of spinal injury, bruising or problems in the area. If in any doubt check with your healthcare practitioner.

Okay, so what happens if you do not have a willing partner? Then, two tennis balls in a sock are going to be your new best friends!

Place two tennis balls in a sock and tie the end tightly.

Lie on your back with knees bent and feet flat on the floor.

Raise your body up slightly and place the balls under the top of the spine.

The spine itself will sit comfortably between each ball.

Pressure should never be applied directly to the bone itself, but to the muscles on either side of the spine.

Lower your weight on to the ball and wriggle around so it massages the neurolymphatic reflex points along each side of the spine.

Alternatively, you can just lie on top of the balls and after about 30 seconds you will begin to feel the back relax and the points 'opening'. Do this down the entire length of the spine, spending a little extra time on any sore spots.

If getting up and down from the floor is not easy for you, an excellent variation [and the one I personally use] is to place the balls on a wall, ideally on a corner, or door jam.

Feet should be placed about 18" away from the wall [the further away the more pressure is applied to the back].

Lean your full body weight against the balls.

Bend knees to manoeuvre them up and down the spine, wriggle around and pay attention to the sore points.

 Sit against the balls on a plane, it helps reduce back pain, you might get a few funny looks but your back will benefit.

COLON HYDROTHERAPY

When you have completed the programme, colonic irrigation can be useful to further cleanse the intestinal tract. It really can be the icing on the cake.

Find a well qualified therapist, ideally through personal recommendation.

http://www.colonic-association.org/ is the site to visit if you would like to know more and to find a therapist, explains how the therapy works and even has a video showing you, tastefully, what to expect.

Always follow a colonic irrigation with live Acidophilus, to repopulate the gut with friendly bacteria.

Body brushing speeds up the elimination of toxins, strengthens the immune system and done regularly, leaves you with extra soft/smooth skin.

Using a *soft* bristle brush[9] use long sweeping strokes, **on dry skin**. Imagine a belt around your waist: everything above that belt you stroke into the armpits and everything below the belt stroke into the groin area.

This is a gentle [yet invigorating] technique – you are not using the brush roughly to encourage blood circulation, rather gently to encourage the lymphatic flow... they are different systems.

Follow with a shower and briskly rub skin with flannel or loofah to remove debris from the skin.

Turbo charge your shower by blowing hot and cold to improve the flow of blood, lymph and the nervous system. It is also said to be great for the immune system. Hot for 3 minutes and then a cold 1 minute blast
repeat a couple of times [if you can].
I wrote the draft of this section last night, it was on my mind, so this morning I walked my talk – brrrrrrrr but it I had forgotten just how invigorating it is – I am definitely reintroducing it into my daily routine!

---

9 Many shops do body brushes, try the Body Shop – just make sure it is SOFT bristle, don't get tempted by other variations.

One evening a week, relax in a hot **Epsom Salt [magnesium sulphate] + Tea Tree bath**. 3 mugs of Epsom Salts and a few drops of good quality, organic tea tree essential oil, in your bath will help draw out further toxins from your body. Soak for 20 minutes then shower off the salts afterwards and go to bed.

FLOWER ESSENCES

STRESS is a major contributing factor with Candida, it weakens every single system of the body thereby allowing the little terror to gain a foothold.

Get tested to see which essence (there are hundreds) would be the most helpful to you at this moment in time; what is stressing you? Are you frustrated or angry? [Both emotions associated with CA].

One excellent 'classic' essence for overall stress is the Australian Bush Essence[10] called BLACK EYED SUSAN.

Start putting 'you' in Number 1 position on your priority list, start self caring; take time out every day for you, some downtime to do what relaxes you: it may be walking the dog or reading a book – enjoy it.

10 www.ausflowers.com.au

A QUICK FIX

When you are walking to work, standing in a queue or doing anything mundane, such as ironing or making the bed, bring all your attention to what you are doing and what you can SEE, HEAR and SMELL. It will bring you right slap bang into the 'present' in a most enjoyable way.

Learning to live in the present moment is one of the most difficult things for us to do but there is an immense freedom when you begin to let go of brooding over the past and worrying about the future – you begin to bring back joy into your life and instantly take the edge of stress.

Words and thoughts are not the only weapons at your disposal. Your ability to visualise, using all your senses can help you win any inner battle. Try this ...

Close your eyes and create a vision, in glorious Technicolor, of yourself, slim, fit, happy, healthy and filled with energy, love and laughter. Involve all the senses – how do you look? Smells? Feelings? Hold it firmly in your mind. Smile and superimpose a huge 'tick' over that picture and, at the same time, say 'YES!' With time, effort and commitment, this vision will become your reality

Teddy Boy Sweep
The instant de-stressor

Deceptively simple and very effective, this technique simply traces part of the Triple Warmer meridian *backwards,* sedating and soothing it to instantly reduce and take the edge of the stress reaction.

You will feel calmer and more able to cope. If you think about it, we do it instinctively, it is a natural movement.

Reducing the debilitating effect of Triple Warmer overwhelm on the Spleen meridian, can strengthen immunity and the ability to metabolise the stress. A definite plus in our battle against CA.

- Place the palms of your hands over your temples, in front of your ears.

- Take a deep breath

- Slide the palms up over and behind the ears, down the neck

- Pause on the area where a necklace would sit, at the back of the neck, take another deep breath and apply slightly more pressure then pull your hands off the body, towards the front.

- Shake your hands off and repeat as many times as necessary until you feel calmer.

As with any condition, you can only heal 100% if your energy is balanced and your 'inner healer' is working to optimum efficiency.

With Candida, it is particularly important to strengthen the LIVER and SPLEEN [immune system], your body needs these two systems to be strong to fight the yeast invader.

There are some basic techniques that you can do, they only take a couple of minutes a day but will deliver huge benefits. Perhaps one of the most effective healing techniques is to maintain a positive attitude, look for the beauty and joy in your life now, smile, laugh for an instant distress.

> Tracing the Regulator Flow
> takes about 30 seconds and helps the other exercises hold.
> Sometimes a visual is far easier to follow – watch my clip on You Tube and see how easy this flow is.[11]

- The regulator flow is the 'co-ordinator'.

- The front (yin) and back (yang) regulator flows influence hormones, chemistry, and circulation as well as the connections among all the systems in the body. They literally turn on and co-ordinate them all.

---

11 If you can't access it directly for some reason, go on my midlife goddess site, I have posted it there.

- Relevant to any auto-immune problem [which is basically where energies are not communicating with each other or adjusting correctly].

- As it runs straight through the thyroid, it always affects it.

- Regulator helps your body adapt to endless assaults of internal and external changes.

- Hormonal imbalances and emotional turmoil can be eased by working with the regulator flow.

- Regulator also establishes harmonies with other people and within the environment.

- It helps you adjust to the new.

- It is essential in dealing with change, be it thrust upon you or elusive.

- Being a 'strangeflow' it helps increase your 'joy in life'.

Activating the Regulator

One of the simplest ways of activating any flow is to trace it. Tracing is done with the open palms of your hands. You either touch the body/clothing or work a couple of inches over it. You can enhance the tracing by using an essential oil mix such as frankincense and lavender or holding a crystal of your choice, but these are not necessary, they are what I respectfully call 'my toy box'.

Trace the front [yin flow] on yourself

- Take a moment to stand tall, centre and earth yourself.

- Rub your hands together, place fingertips between the eyebrows.

- Trace a HEART around the outside of the face

- That heart sits on a STICK running down the front of the throat

- Cross your arms like a genie in front of you at chest level

- Uncross them, running your palms up to your shoulders so that your forearms are in a pharaoh position, i.e. crossed over the chest.

- Bring hands down to the side of the breasts – a la Marilyn Munroe [or Katie Price]

- Smile and move hands down the front of the body – 'Oh, I'm so beautiful!'

- Move over the ribs, pelvis, thighs, knees, shins and the top of the feet, pause here

- Squeeze lateral and medial sides together [pressure on Bladder and Spleen meridians]

- End by brushing off the feet

- Come up slowly, let your abdominal muscles do the work, vertebrae by vertebrae – you may also like to swing your torso slightly in a loose figure 8.

Tracing the back flow – yang

- Palms on temples

- Do the Teddy Boy Sweep – move your palms up over the top and behind the ears and off the shoulders

- Cross your arms like a genie again, clasp the upper arm a little higher up – say an inch.

- Run your hands up the arms to the shoulders so that your forearms are again in the pharaoh position

- Then into Marilyn position on either side of your breasts

- Move hands onto the back as high as is comfortable

- Trace down the back – in at the waist and out at the hips

- Down the back of the legs and off the little toes

- Come up slowly, figure 8'ing as you come up [this helps reinforce Strangeflow energies]

Finish by placing your hands in a 'prayer' position, i.e. palms together. Place them in front of your chest over the Thymus area and gently push into the Thymus for ten seconds, then release and say 'thank you'.

I often end my energy exercises with this short pose as it is relaxing and gives the body a few seconds to integrate the corrections you have made. I also love the fact that in the Indian tradition, it is believed you access your soul through this spot.

The 4 THUMPS

just 5 seconds each one

I have been talking a lot about 'energy', what exactly do I mean?

Energy is a life-force that flows through and around our bodies. It is the blueprint, the infrastructure, the invisible foundation for the health of your body.[12]

It is not a figment of an overactive bohemian imagination but can be clearly measured by scientific equipment [e.g. MRI or EEG] and captured by Kirlian photography. Fascinating research is taking place right now regarding the harnessing of the 'energy' of thought, to a prosthetic limb to control its movement.

Like radio, TV, cell phone waves, the wind and electricity, energy cannot be seen with the naked eye, but it is most definitely there.

It exists and without it, we would not.

The foundation stone of good health is a free flowing energy system. If the 'flow' is disturbed in any way, due

---

12 Curtis and Hurtak propose, the meridian system may be a distinct energy system that "functions alongside the accepted blood circulatory, lymphatic, and nervous systems," capable of reading, coding, and transmitting information from one part of the body to another and providing "an underlying template for the physical body. They believe it operates on a distinct energetic spectrum whose movement is more like an energy wave than a tube or vessel. Supporting the hypothesis that this energy system impacts biological processes, abundant anecdotal and limited empirical evidence suggests that disruption in a meridian pathway precedes (and, again, thus predicts) disease in specific organs served by that meridian, and that meridians whose energies are disrupted can be treated for therapeutic benefit.

to stress or trauma it has repercussions on the physical body: lowered immunity, increased food intolerances, increased vulnerability to CA, diminished ability to cope with the challenges of life, fatigue, lethargy, depression, lack of efficiency of the major organs and systems – it hits every single part of your body. The effects may be subtle at first but cumulative and over years can contribute to ill health.

There are different energy systems in the body that work in pure synergy. As you get to know your energies and more importantly energy disruptions and how to correct them, you can often prevent physical symptoms manifesting. For the purpose of this book, we are working with the basic 'foundation energies', simple, but profoundly effective in your battle with CA.

The body has remarkable self-healing powers but these can only achieve their full potential if the energies are balanced and free flowing. So, to release your 'Inner Healer', start paying attention to your flows!

There are 'meridians' of energy running through the body, think of them as motorways connecting the different organs and systems. Energy should run in a specific direction along each channel. However, due to stress, physical or emotional exhaustion or trauma, energy can sometimes flip into reverse and literally run backwards along the meridians, going the wrong way up that motorway and causing chaos.

If this happens you may:

- lack focus/concentration/clarity of thought
- feel tired

- possibly be depressed most of the time and life can seem as if you are pushing water uphill

- Your immunity will be compromised resulting in frequent, niggling coughs and colds

- None of your systems will operate to full potential

- Never feel 100% well

If that sounds familiar, maybe your energies are 'reversed'.

Get back in the right lane, flip your energies back into the correct direction with the following technique [the 4 thumps], it takes all of 20 seconds. Do it 5-6 times a day and see if you feel better and life seems a bit easier.

Form your thumb and first two fingers into a triad and firmly massage or tap the points described below.

If you have long nails, simply improvise and use your knuckles. Don't forget to breath and smile while you tap.

The benefits of this simple exercise include:–

- 'Flips' energy into forward flow.

- Jump-starts and energises the entire system.

- Balances disruptions caused by travelling, especially through time zones. [A great one to do during a flight and when you step off the plane].

- Brings clarity to thought.

- Improves focus and concentration.

- Brings a flow back into your life.

- Temporarily energises the eyes, useful if you are tired but still have a few more miles to drive.

You will be tapping and therefore stimulating the 27th acupuncture point on each Kidney meridian. These important points act as 'junction boxes' for other meridians.

They are located near the 'right angle' where the collar and breast bones meet. You will feel two natural indentations that may be slightly tender when you press them.

Don't worry if you can't find the exact points, you know the approximate area, so tap around and you will get them, as with all energy work, it is about intention and attention.

Breathe, fully moving your rib cage and diaphragm. Smile and tap for 5 seconds.

THE TARZEN THUMP!

Benefits of this second thump include:

- Stimulates the Thymus gland.

- Supports the Immune System.

- Helps cope with the body's stress response and negative emotional energies.

- Stimulates overall energy and vitality – primates will thump this gland to increase their strength before mating or fighting.

- Places the body in a temporary state of 'balance'.

 You will be tapping over the Thymus Gland[13] which is located in the middle of your chest – exactly where Tarzan thumps, in fact rather than tapping; you could clench your fists and thump your chest like Tarzan!

Breathe, smile and tap/thump for 5 seconds.

13 The Australian psychiatrist, Dr John Diamond [Your Body Doesn't Lie] www.drjohndiamond.com – made a study of the Thymus gland and suggests we 'waltz' the thymus, i.e. tap lightly to the waltz rhythm ... 123 123 123, smile and look at something beautiful while you are tapping to increase the effectiveness of the exercise.

Benefits of monkey thumping include:–

- Boosts Immune System and general energy levels.

- Increases your ability to accept/metabolise changes.

- Balances blood chemistry.

- Aids detoxification of the body.

- Helps metabolise and absorb nutrients.

- Improves absorption of supplements [tap for 5 seconds before and after taking them].

You will be massaging/tapping/thumping the 21st acupressure points on each Spleen meridian. These are located on the side of the ribcage, roughly where the bottom line of a bra would sit [see photo]. You will know when you hit on them as they will be tender.

Once located, use your clenched fists to massage, tap or thump firmly the points for a minimum of 5 seconds.

Breathe and smile.

You can also work on the Spleen lymphatic points: simply lean back slightly, opening up the ribcage and tap round from Sp21 to underneath each breast in line with the nipples.

- Relieves anxiety

- Helps you begin to trust in the mystery of life

- Helps in letting issues pass through, be digested and released

- Balanced Stomach energy encourages you to pay attention to self-care

- Helps achieve a clear thought process.

Called the 'Great Bone Hole' they are located slightly below the apex of your cheeks when you smile, in line with your eye and the edge of your nostril.

Again, do for 5 seconds.

CROSS CRAWL – 20 seconds

- Do you feel tired for no real reason?

- Do you have a tendency to pessimism or depression?

- Are you slowly becoming a lethargic sloth?

- Is motivating yourself to do anything a major task?

- Do you find your memory is not what it was?

- Do you lack a
  certain clarity and focus in your thinking?

- Rather than
  feel energised by exercise does it tend to tire
  you?

- Do you feel you are only operating at about 50%
  efficiency?

- Are you constantly getting niggling coughs and
  colds?

- Do you feel that your senses are less acute?

If the answer is 'yes' to any of the above, read on. The Cross Crawl could definitely be of help to you.

The body functions with crossing patterns, curves, roundness and above all, flow. There are very few sharp edges in the human body.

This technique is based on the fact that the left hemisphere of the brain needs to send information to the right side of the body and the right hemisphere to the left side. If either of these 'communication tracts' are not adequately flowing and open then it will be impossible to access the brain's full capacity or the body's full intelligence.

The bottom line is: when our energies are crossed every system in the body and the body's healing abilities is encouraged to optimum efficiency, we are literally healthier. However, when the energies are not crossed, the healing abilities are dramatically reduced.

We are born with the energies running in a parallel pattern, homolaterally[14] down the body but when, as babies, we start to crawl; the crossover pattern and left/right brain integration really begins to take form. This is why children who do not crawl enough can develop learning difficulties. So don't just plonk your baby/grandchild in a bouncer, let it roam wild – the crawling action will enable enhanced brain function.

Back to us as adults: Nature intended that we cross crawl naturally during the course of each day: walking, running, swimming are all natural ways of consolidating that crossing pattern. However, contemporary lifestyles are increasingly sedentary. In addition, fashion footwear can prohibit good posture and, we carry heavy shoulder bags, briefcases or shopping bags which all inhibit the natural flow of the movement.

Needless to say any stress or trauma in our life can throw the pattern back into homolateral. Our body will give us hints when this happens – for example stop reading right now and see if any 'body part' is crossed – wrists, arms, ankles, legs? This is a message that the body needs/ wants to cross its energies, it yearns to run at full efficiency, it seeks balance to do so.

Body language specialists say crossed arms mean a closed off/ defensive stance, but in reality, from an energetic standpoint, it can also mean that you are trying to cross the energies, albeit unconsciously, so that you can truly understand what is being said to you.

So, to summarise; doing a CROSS CRAWL can improve left and right brain integration and encourage energies to cross.

---

14 We use the word homolateral to indicate this parallel patterning.
II

This in turn can:–

- Greatly improve the body's natural healing ability.

- Enhance the absorption of vitamin supplementation.

- Relieve fatigue, exhaustion and lack of motivation.

- Bring clarity to your thinking.

- Help your whole system function more efficiently.

- Improve co-ordination.

- Reduce certain learning difficulties.

- Stimulate memory.

- Pump lymphatic and cerebrospinal fluid.

- Help you feel more balanced, motivated and energised.

- Harmonise energies and increase natural self healing abilities.

- Ease depression.

- Support the immune system.

- Support and help
make more effective any other treatments you may
be receiving from your healthcare practitioner.

1. Lift your right arm and right leg together. Then lift your left arm and left leg together. Do you remember the Thunderbird puppets! Repeat a few times/15 seconds or so. This reflects the homolateral, parallel patterning which your brain will recognise and feel comfortable with if your energies are not crossing.

2. Now lift your right arm and left leg together [see photo on the right above] followed by left arm and right leg. i.e. diagonal/opposites together. Repeat a few times/15 seconds. This represents the cross over pattern and may feel uncomfortable until your energies reprogramme themselves into a crossing pattern.

3. Repeat

ALWAYS end on the cross over pattern

and do a few extra 'crosses' to integrate the reprogramming.

Cross Crawl every time you are waiting for the kettle to boil — let it slip effortlessly into your life and become a habit. It will be subtle, but you will definitely begin to feel the benefits within a couple of weeks.

Over the following months the body will begin to hold on to the crossover patterning as it becomes more ingrained. Any stress or trauma may send you into homolateral, but if you are cross crawling every day, you will never be in that state for more than 24 hours and therefore should not suffer from any associated symptoms.

If you have problems with mobility and cannot stand or balance to do this exercise, it can be done sitting down or even on your back in bed.

When you are striding out on a walk, make sure your body is moving in the cross/diagonal patterning and you have thumped K27 to get your energies running in the right direction – takes seconds but you will get dramatically more benefit from the exercise.

[otherwise you could be literally walking against your own flow of energy which will tire rather than refresh you.

LYMPHATIC POINTS FOR LIVER AND LARGE INTESTINE

I want to keep things as simple as possible, so as not to overload you and what could be simpler than massaging the Liver lymphatic points. They lie directly under your right breast, exactly where a bra underwire sits.

Massage firmly, you will probably wince and curse me, but tenderness is a sign that you need to stimulate these points, there will come a day when you are massaging firmly and there will be no pain whatsoever – that is the day you know your Liver is balanced.

The large intestine points are equally easy to locate – sitting down the outside of the thigh, exactly where the seam of your trousers runs. Massage very firmly from hip to knee on both thighs.

Massage firmly for ten seconds twice a day. Maybe after cleaning your teeth, put a post it note on your mirror to remind yourself.

Recruit the power of the Tibetan Figure 8

This technique has helped me in many aspects of health care over the past years – deceptively simple it has been used for centuries in the Tibetan healing traditions where they believe that 8 is the sign for infinity and has a healing power all of its own. All you have to do is trace an imaginary Figure 8 [horizontal or vertical, it doesn't matter] over your abdominal area. Trace for a minute to release the healing power of 8.

--oOo--

To recap, you will be:

- changing your diet,

- taking key supplementations,

- doing a simple daily energy medicine routine to get your basic energies balanced so they support your self-healing abilities.

- reducing your stress levels and

- remaining positive.

Sounds so easy writing this short paragraph but it will be a challenge so don't forget the secret tap [on the top of your hand].

OKAY, you've got rid of it. It was a long, hard fight. What do you do to prevent it coming back?

First and foremost, don't go back to the bad habits that caused your immunity to lower and the yeast invader to dominate.

Learn how to reduce your stress reaction.

Review your lifestyle and find a healthy, practical one that you can live with easily.

Be discerning, it would be impossible to live on the CA programme for life – be realistic and honest with yourself about the time and commitment you can give to a new lifestyle plan, you will then find it easier to follow the plan long-term.

In summary, you should consider including in your general lifestyle, the following changes.

- The basic energy exercises in this booklet. They will benefit you, not just in the battle against CA but also give you firm energetic foundations that will support you in all challenges. The regulator flow is particularly useful in helping you regulate and adapt to change.

- Physical exercise plan – maybe it's just a brisk daily walk, but your body will benefit from moving, especially in a way that you enjoy.

- Healthy nutritious diet that suits your individual body chemistry

- Sensible supplementation

- Higher water intake

- A stress control technique that you enjoy and works for you.

You should be avoiding excessive:

- Sugars,

- Chemical rich foods,

- Alcohol,

- Caffeine

- Antibiotics. *If you do take them, supplement with friendly bacteria so that a yeast infection does not have the opportunity of getting a hold.*

- Drugs

- Foods that contain antibiotics, preservatives and chemicals.

ONE FINAL WORD

Before you start, get organised, fill your kitchen with things you <u>can</u> eat, every time you open your fridge door there should be some real goodies that you enjoy staring right back at you.

Get all the information you need easily to hand. Be clear in what you are going to achieve, after all, you can't reach a goal unless you set one. Try and clear your diary of possible situations that will overly 'tempt' you.

Create a positive frame of mind, don't view yourself as a victim of the diet, you have been a victim of Candida and now you are taking control, you will soon be free of its painful tyranny.

**And remember
It is not for life but it will change your life!**

MADISON KING

writer and teacher of energy medicine

Madison's Medicine is a unique fusion of energy and body work, flower essences, lifestyle advice and commonsense – providing essential, everyday, practical tools for a healthier and happier you.

Many moons ago Madison was involved in the heart of London advertising, becoming a successful international board director. However, she realised, after a few ambition fuelled years, that she wanted her life to take a different direction and shocked everyone by giving up the BMW, Armani suits and Gucci briefcase, becoming a student again.

She trained in massage, sports massage, aromatherapy, Indian head massage, reflexology, trager, nutrition, flower essences, crystals, radionics ... A true workshop groupie, she filled a wall with qualifications but could not find what she had been seeking; she couldn't even really define it ... until, through divine synchronicity, she met Donna Eden in London through a mutual friend. Within no time at all she was in Ashland in Donna's backyard with about four other students, eagerly learning about energy – this was more than two decades ago, so no information highway was available in those days and ever the thirsty student she drank in everything she could on these visits, rushing back to London to experiment on her long suffering clients!

Over the years she crossed the ocean many times learning from Donna and also John Thie [Touch for Health].

She then began to teach Donna's work in the UK, USA, Gozo, Malta, Italy, Egypt and many other locations around the world, she has appeared on national television, radio and press promoting EEM. She has lectured at Westminster and Oxford universities and at the key Mind Body Spirit Festivals in London and Wales.

In 2006 she gave up a thriving practice in Central London and now divides her time between the Isle of Wight and the Andalucían town of Nerja in Southern Spain.

Just about to enter her 7th decade, she has set up and is running Donna Eden's training in Europe – based just outside London... a long way from those days in Donna's back yard!

Her focus is on promoting Donna's work in Europe and also writing and teaching her own version: Madison's Medicine, which based on Eden Energy Medicine also weaves in many other natural health threads, giving people simple yet powerful tools to enhance their quality of life on every single level.

As we enter unprecedented waters on this planet, it can be empowering to know that there is always something YOU can do to improve any situation, challenge or trauma that life throws into your path.

"Madison is an extraordinary woman and healer. She carries an essence of the highest quality and caring, of camaraderie of spirit, wisdom, compassion and depth of understanding of the healing realms. To train with her is something you will never regret"
Donna Eden – Eden Energy Medicine

Madison can be contacted:

www.madisonking.com
www.midlifegoddess.ning.com
madisonking@hotmail.com

My special thanks to Donna Eden.[15]
Without her friendship and generous, unselfish
sharing of her vast knowledge, I would not be who I
am today and you would not be reading this book.
(Footnotes)

---

15 www.innersource.net